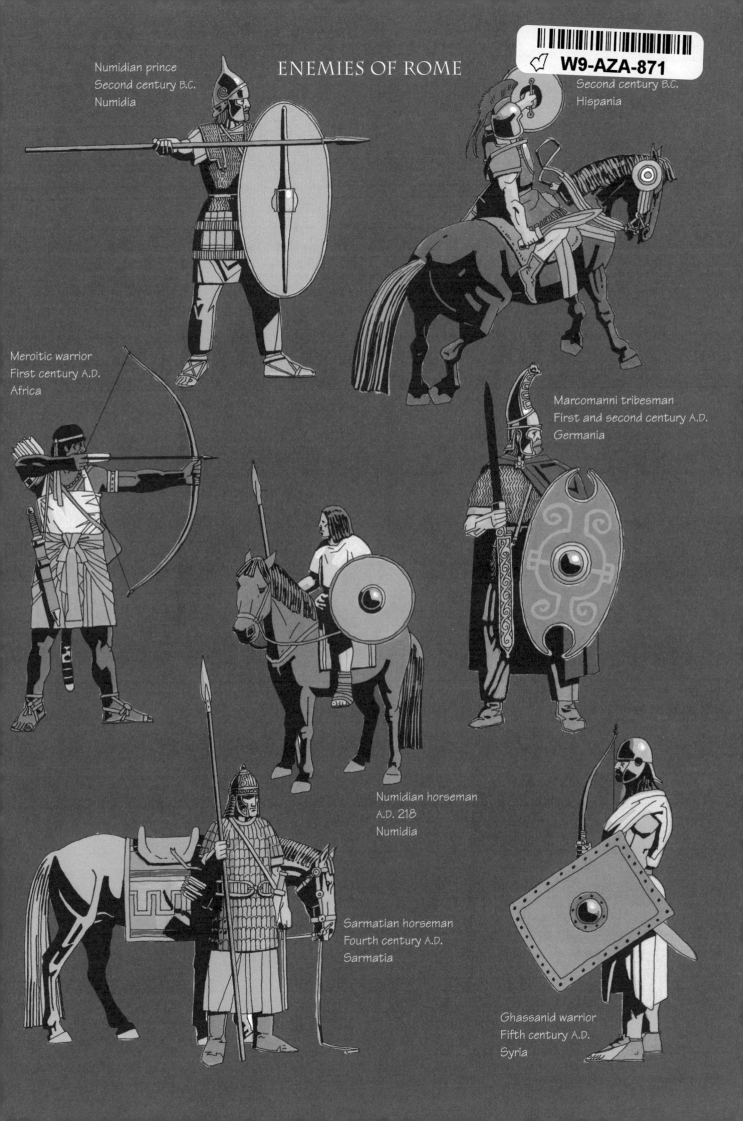

ENEMIES OF ROME

Numidian prince
Second century B.C.
Numidia

Second century B.C.
Hispania

Meroitic warrior
First century A.D.
Africa

Marcomanni tribesman
First and second century A.D.
Germania

Numidian horseman
A.D. 218
Numidia

Sarmatian horseman
Fourth century A.D.
Sarmatia

Ghassanid warrior
Fifth century A.D.
Syria

THE ROMAN ARMY

The Legendary Soldiers Who Created an Empire

DYAN BLACKLOCK

ILLUSTRATIONS BY

DAVID KENNETT

Walker & Company ◉ New York

For Jordan, my soldier boy —D. B.

For Carol McLean-Carr, dear friend, with love —D. K.

David Kennett acknowledges a debt to the works of Angus McBride and Frank Frazzetta.
Special thanks to Professor Malcolm Cooper, Ritsumeikan Asia Pacific University,
and to Dr. Anne Geddes, Centre for European Studies, University of Adelaide.

First published in the United States of America in 2004 by
Walker Publishing Company, Inc.

Published simultaneously in Canada by Fitzhenry and Whiteside, Markham,
Ontario L3R 4T8

Originally published in Australia in 2004 by Omnibus Books, an imprint of
Scholastic Australia Pty. Ltd.

For information about permission to reproduce selections from this book, write to
Permissions, Walker & Company, 104 Fifth Avenue, New York, New York 10011

Library of Congress Cataloging-in-Publication Data
Blacklock, Dyan.
  The Roman Army / Dyan Blacklock ; [illustrations by] David Kennett.
    p. cm.
  Summary: An illustrated history of the Roman Army, including information
  about its composition, organization, training, methods, weapons, and campaigns.
  Includes bibliographical references and index.
  ISBN 0-8027-8896-3 (HC) — ISBN 0-8027-8897-1 (RE)
  1. Rome–Army–Juvenile literature. [1. Rome–Army. 2. Military art and science–
  Rome.] I. Kennett, David, 1959- ill. II. Title.
U35.B58 2004
355'.00937'6—dc22   2003057574

The artist used technical pen, Fineliner, and markers for the line work and
acrylic paint on Arches watercolor paper for the color illustrations in this book.
Digital coloring, book design, and typography by Eija Murch-Lempinen.

Visit Walker & Company's Web site at www.walkeryoungreaders.com

Printed in Singapore

2 4 6 8 10 9 7 5 3

The Roman Empire was one of the largest and most successful empires of all time. It lasted for hundreds of years, from 27 B.C. to A.D. 476, and at the height of its power it extended from Syria in the east and northern Africa in the south, to Britain and Germany in the north. Such a broad and diverse empire was difficult to control. This complex and dangerous work was the job of one of the most fearsome forces the world has ever seen—the Roman army.

Britannia

Germania

Oceanus
Atlanticus

Gallia

Itali

Hispania

Rom

Numidia

THE
ROMAN
EMPIRE,
A.D. 117

Sarmatia

Pontus Euxinus

Dacia

Armenia

Asia Minor

Achaea

Syria

Judaea

Arabia

Mare Internum

Aegyptus

The Roman army maintained a system of forts to monitor traffic in and out of the conquered territories that made up the empire.

A Roman fort contained everything that was needed to keep the soldiers healthy, well trained, and properly equipped.

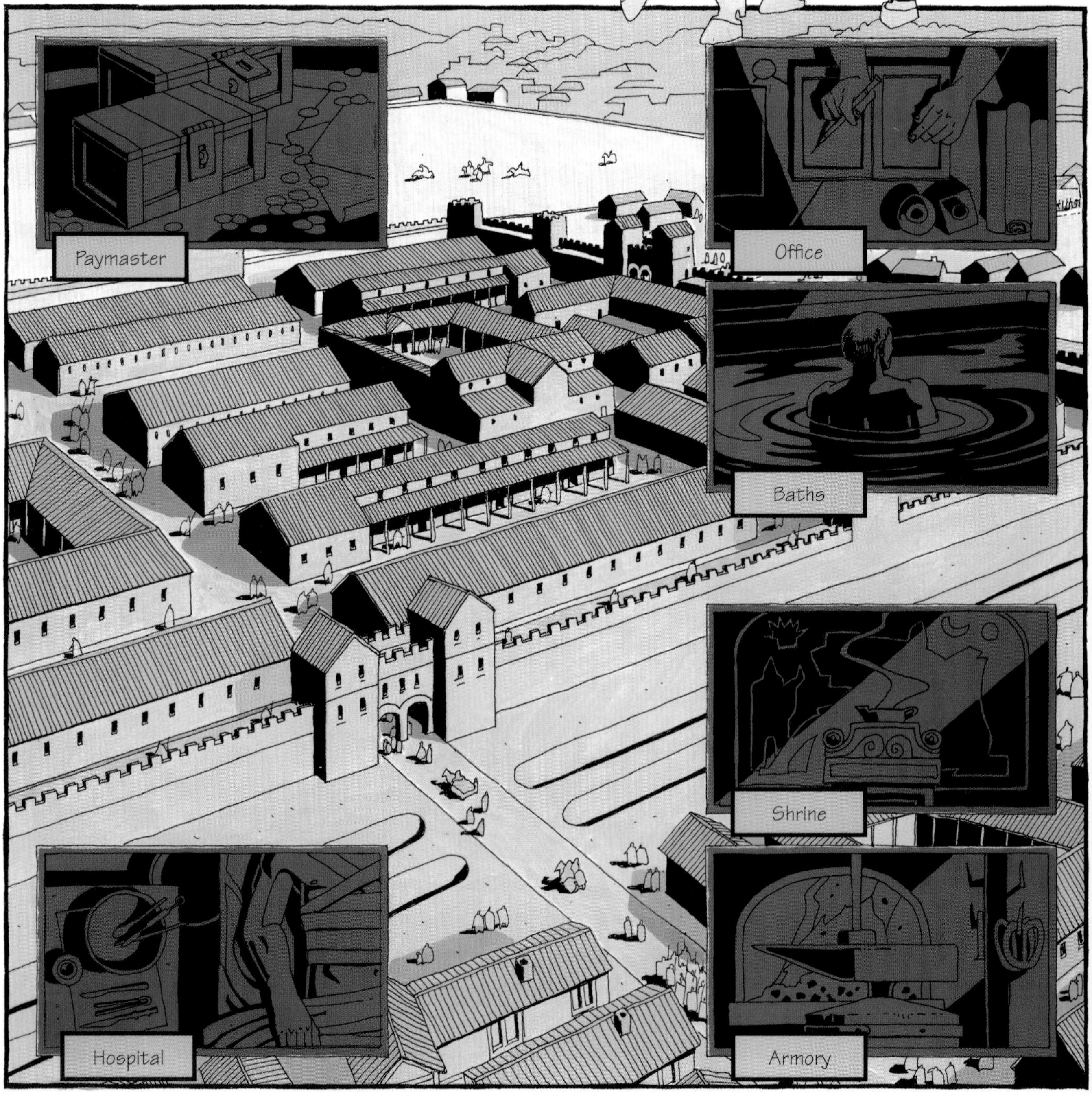

Paymaster

Office

Baths

Shrine

Hospital

Armory

Traders, artisans, and soldiers' slaves and families followed the Roman army as it traveled. Permanent forts had a *vicus,* or civilian settlement, where soldiers could spend their money. Roman soldiers were paid. In early times they might have been provided with salt, which was a valuable commodity. The word *salary* comes from *sal,* the Latin word for "salt." The word *soldier,* in turn, comes from an old French word for "salary."

THE ROMAN LEGIONS

At the time of the Roman Empire's greatest power, its army was an effective and professional force. It comprised a number of legions, each with around 5,500 men.

There were ten cohorts in a legion. The elite troops formed the First Cohort, which was double the size of the other nine cohorts. There were six centuries in the other cohorts, each led by a centurion. During this period, a centurion commanded eighty men.

 The **general** was appointed by the Roman emperor. He was often a senator rather than a career soldier and relied on his senior centurions for advice.

 The **senior tribune** was second in command. Five **junior tribunes** were responsible for the legionaries' welfare and daily routine.

 The **centurion** was a tough, experienced soldier. Centurions were the backbone of the army.

 The **century optio** was appointed by the centurion to take command if the centurion fell in battle.

A **legionary** was always a Roman citizen. Legionaries enlisted for twenty years.

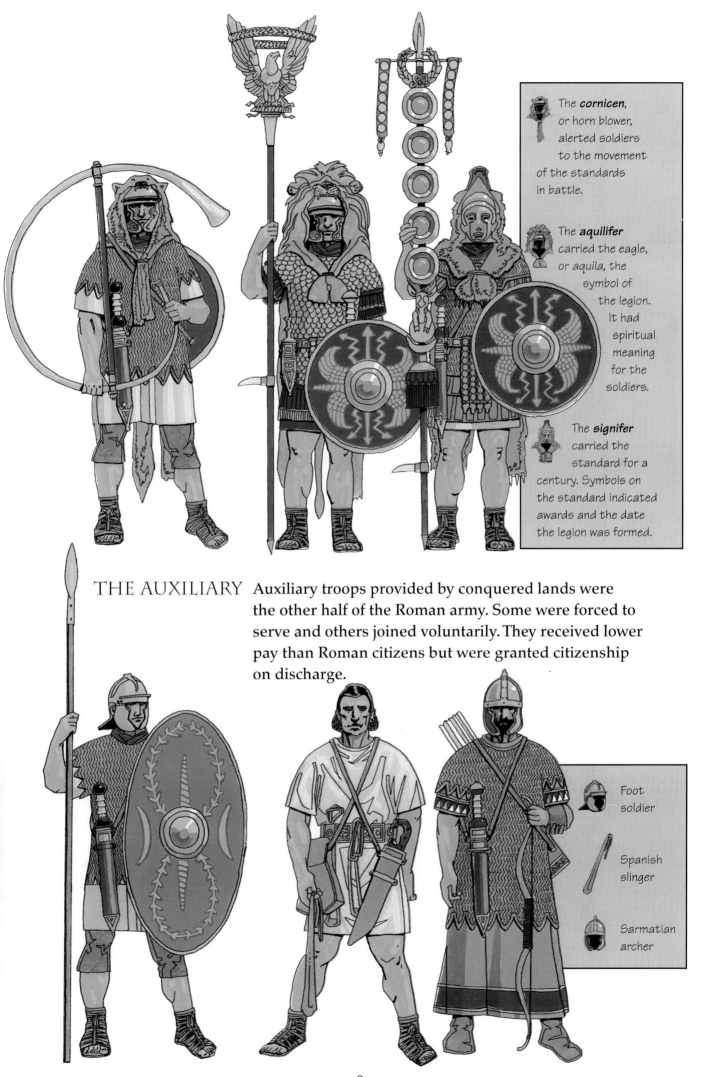

The **cornicen**, or horn blower, alerted soldiers to the movement of the standards in battle.

The **aquilifer** carried the eagle, or aquila, the symbol of the legion. It had spiritual meaning for the soldiers.

The **signifer** carried the standard for a century. Symbols on the standard indicated awards and the date the legion was formed.

THE AUXILIARY Auxiliary troops provided by conquered lands were the other half of the Roman army. Some were forced to serve and others joined voluntarily. They received lower pay than Roman citizens but were granted citizenship on discharge.

Foot soldier

Spanish slinger

Sarmatian archer

Dense forests provided perfect cover for enemies hoping to ambush the army.

In extending the control of the empire, the Roman army marched into enemy territory, building roads and forts and establishing supply lines as it went.

Once the land was conquered, road building began.

The pioneers worked ahead of the main army, clearing a path to avoid ambush.

Most soldiers hated the heavy work of road building.

The Roman navy supported the army on campaign, transporting men, animals, and supplies on fleets of ships stationed at sea and along major rivers.

The navy also played an important role in the life of the empire by keeping trade routes open. Grain transported from Egypt by sea was essential for feeding the population of Rome.

Legionaries carried a variety of gear. Weighing around 66 pounds (30 kilograms), this gear could include shovels and stakes as well as rations, cooking equipment, and clothing. Soldiers on a campaign marched more than five hours a day, covering up to 22 miles (36 kilometers).

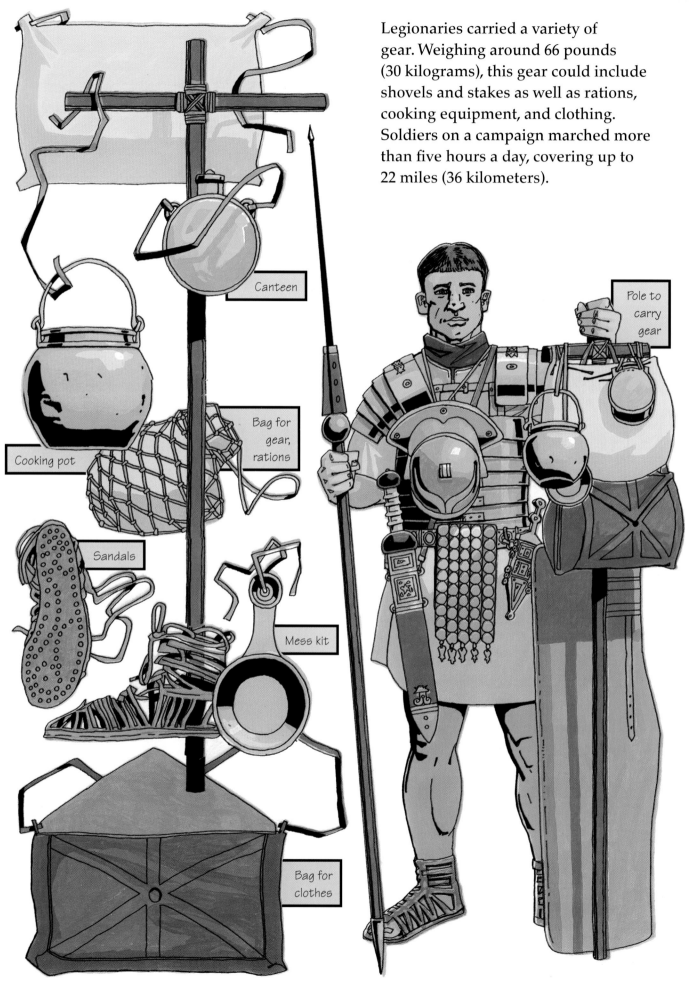

Canteen

Cooking pot

Bag for gear, rations

Sandals

Mess kit

Pole to carry gear

Bag for clothes

The entire army on a march could have stretched out over 12 miles (20 kilometers). Auxiliary foot scouts, marching ahead of the main troops, acted as the eyes and ears of the legion. Legions marched six men abreast where possible.

Cavalry horses were hardy animals of about 13 or 14 hands (one hand is equal to approximately four inches).

Celtic-style helmet. Celtic armorers made helmets for the Roman army.

Chain-mail armor was constructed from metal rings riveted together.

THE CAVALRY

A small number of Roman cavalry traveled in the main army. In early times, the cavalry was recruited from among wealthy Romans who could provide and maintain the animals and equipment required.

Later, Celtic, German, and North African horsemen were recruited as auxiliary cavalry. They were given the dangerous task of scouting. Working away from the main army, they searched out enemy groups and reported back on troop movements.

Enemy captives were taken to the main army for questioning.

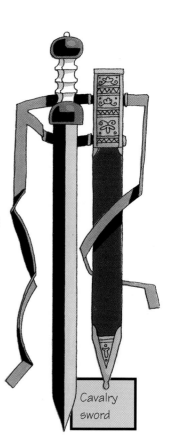

Cavalry sword

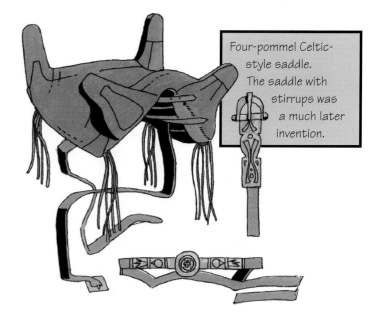

Four-pommel Celtic-style saddle. The saddle with stirrups was a much later invention.

ROMAN ARMS AND ARMOR

Roman armor was both beautiful and practical and often highly ornate. As a result of close observation of the weapons and armor used by its enemies, the Roman army adapted for its own use such things as chain mail, saddles, and helmets from the Celts. From the Spanish they took the shortsword and the legionary dagger.

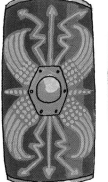

Shields were made from three layers of wooden strips, glued together and covered with hide or canvas. The edges were bound with iron.

Roman armor was made from separate plates riveted to internal straps. Being light and flexible, it was comfortable to wear.

Pilum, or javelin

Dagger

Groin guard

The gladius was modeled on the Spanish shortsword

Military belt ends

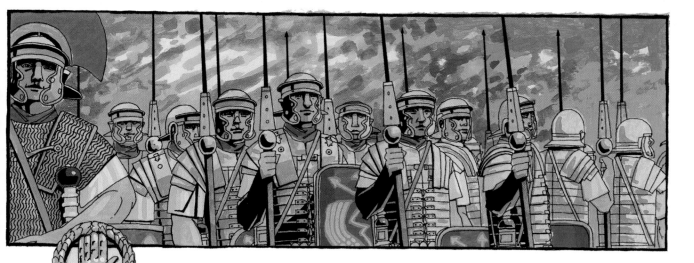

Roman generals, although not always soldiers by training, were always among the front ranks of troops in battle. The best generals had the full support of their men, who could be fanatically loyal. They led by example, and in doing so inspired their men. Naturally, soldiers were keen to follow successful generals who looked after them and won battles with the fewest casualties.

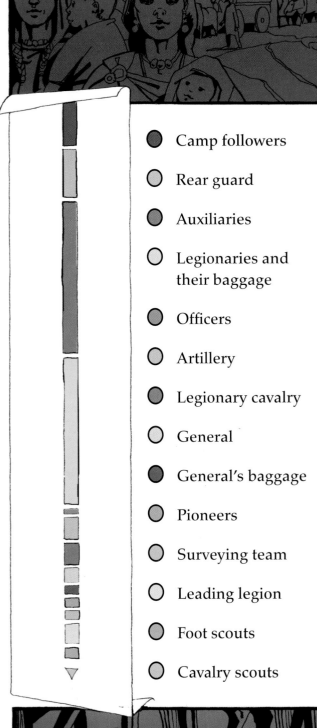

- ● Camp followers
- ○ Rear guard
- ● Auxiliaries
- ○ Legionaries and their baggage
- ● Officers
- ○ Artillery
- ● Legionary cavalry
- ○ General
- ● General's baggage
- ○ Pioneers
- ○ Surveying team
- ○ Leading legion
- ● Foot scouts
- ○ Cavalry scouts

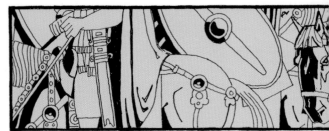

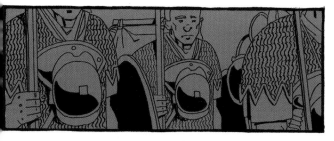

As the army snaked its way through the countryside, it observed a strict marching order. Following behind were slave traders, servants, merchants, baggage handlers, and prostitutes. Soldiers were not allowed to marry, but their common-law wives and children followed them on campaign. Camp followers were sometimes captured and killed by the enemy.

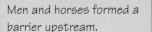

Men and horses formed a barrier upstream.

Rivers presented significant obstacles to the progress of an army. Crossing them could be a long and difficult process that left the army vulnerable to attack.

Where a river could be forded, part of the cavalry would string out across the river upstream, breaking the force of the current and making the passage across easier.

Downstream, the remaining cavalry waited to retrieve men or equipment lost while crossing.

Foot soldiers waded across with their clothes and armor packed on their shields.

Soldiers could put on their own armor, but it was quicker if two comrades helped each other.

Armor was fastened with either buckles or hooks and loops.

On coming to a river that was too deep to ford, army engineers would decide whether to construct a pontoon or pile bridge to cross it.

A pontoon bridge required small boats, ropes, and timber. The boats were anchored into position with wicker cages filled with rocks. Timbers spanned the gaps between the boats, and planks were laid across them to form a roadway.

Pile bridges were made from iron-tipped wooden piles rammed about 39 feet (12 meters) apart into the riverbed by a pile driver. Cross beams formed a series of trestles that supported a roadway.

Wicker cages filled with rocks were lowered onto the riverbed to anchor a pontoon bridge.

A pile driver mounted on a raft drove timber poles into the riverbed for a pile bridge.

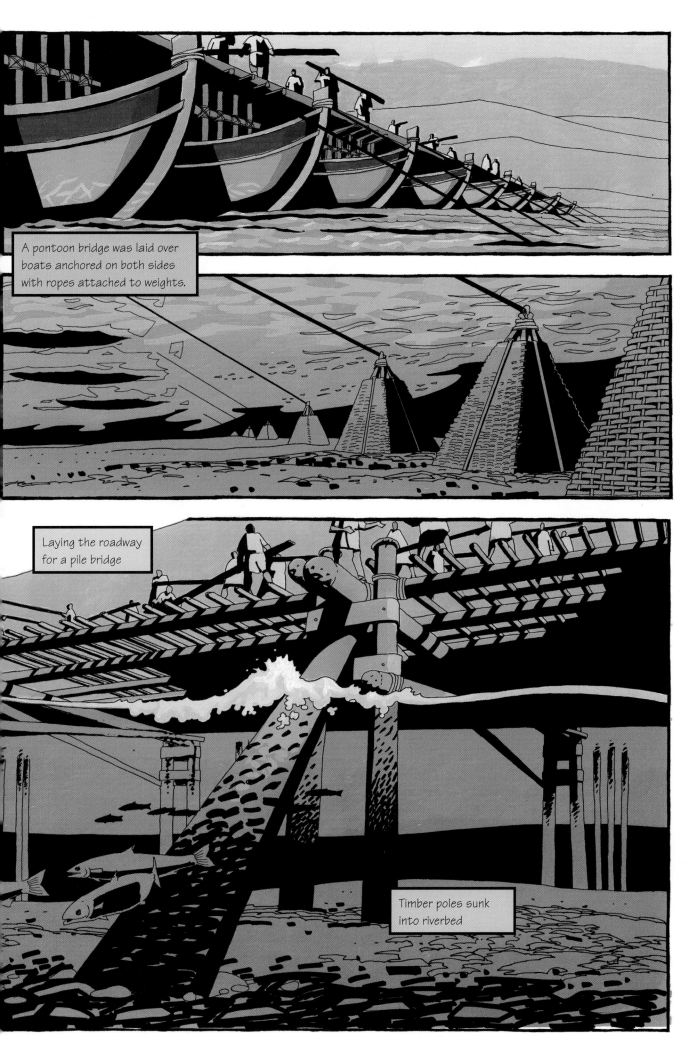

A pontoon bridge was laid over boats anchored on both sides with ropes attached to weights.

Laying the roadway for a pile bridge

Timber poles sunk into riverbed

23

The Roman army was forced to engage the enemy on many types of terrain and in varied climates. The empire included countries as far apart geographically as Britain and North Africa, and so its army marched and fought in heat and cold, in mountainous areas or deserts. Legionaries marched in harsh conditions, although campaigning troops traveled less often in winter, when food was scarce. Soldiers were expected to be uncomplaining and to accept their lot.

Enduring the extreme weather conditions and the difficult terrain of deserts and rocky, mountainous areas was part of a soldier's life.

One general further toughened his men by forcing them to spend the winter in freezing conditions. With little to keep them warm, men could suffer frostbite or even freeze to death while on guard duty.

Roman soldiers were expected to train constantly, often marching long distances even when not under battle conditions. Constant physical exertion made Rome's fighting forces hard and strong—a formidable enemy.

After each day's march, the army constructed a camp, identical in layout to every other marching camp, and sent soldiers out to forage for food and fuel. Each campsite was preselected by survey teams, which had already laid out the perimeter and the streets with flags and pegs.

The surveyor aligned flags using a *groma*, a shaft topped by two crosspieces of metal. A plumb line hung from each of the four ends of the crosspieces. Surveyors took a sight across opposite plumb lines.

The general's tent was always put up first, on a site from which there was the best view.

Legionaries dug an outer ditch, using this earth to form a protective barrier called a rampart topped by a palisade, or fence, of wooden stakes.

When the camp was completed, soldiers marched to their century's tent street and pitched their tents. The next job was to prepare and cook their food.

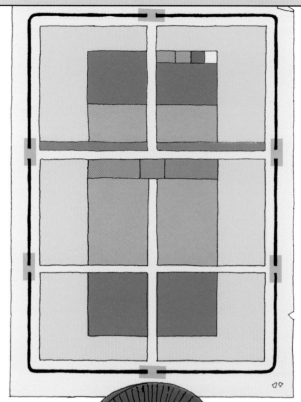

A century's tent street consisted of ten eight-man tents made of goat hide. At the end of the line was a larger tent for the centurion, and the century had its own area for baggage, mules, and gear. Each group of eight men slept, ate, trained, and fought together for the entire twenty years of their service, and it was little wonder that they were so easily able to construct a camp—even in the dark! Soldiers went to bed fully dressed so that they were ready for action in case of enemy attack.

Meticulous organization and planning were key to carrying out the complex task of building and operating a camp.

Supplying food for the army was a massive job and was critical to the success of army operations. Basic campaign rations were simple, the staple being grain cooked into porridge or baked into bread on the campfire. Vegetables, meat, or sour wine or vinegar were welcome additions to a soldier's rations when they could be provided locally.

Men cooked for themselves in eight-man tent groups.

The Romans forced conquered peoples to provide them with food.

In enemy territories where the army was forced to forage for food, attacks on troops engaged in this activity were not uncommon. Guards were assigned to accompany men sent to hunt for food. Roman commanders on campaign were careful to guard supply lines and to establish that there was enough food available in the territory through which the army was traveling. They might also rely on their allies to provide food or exact it from conquered peoples as tribute.

Soldiers foraging for food also raided local houses, farms, or villages.

As well as being highly trained killers, legionaries were skilled carpenters, earthworkers, and builders. As soon as scouts sighted enemy troops, elaborate defenses were quickly constructed for the marching camp. Half the infantry and all the cavalry drew up in battle order in front of the enemy. Other legionaries dug in behind, creating deeper ditches and higher palisades than normal with which to fortify the camp. Fortifications could be completed in two hours, and baggage trains were quickly moved up behind them.

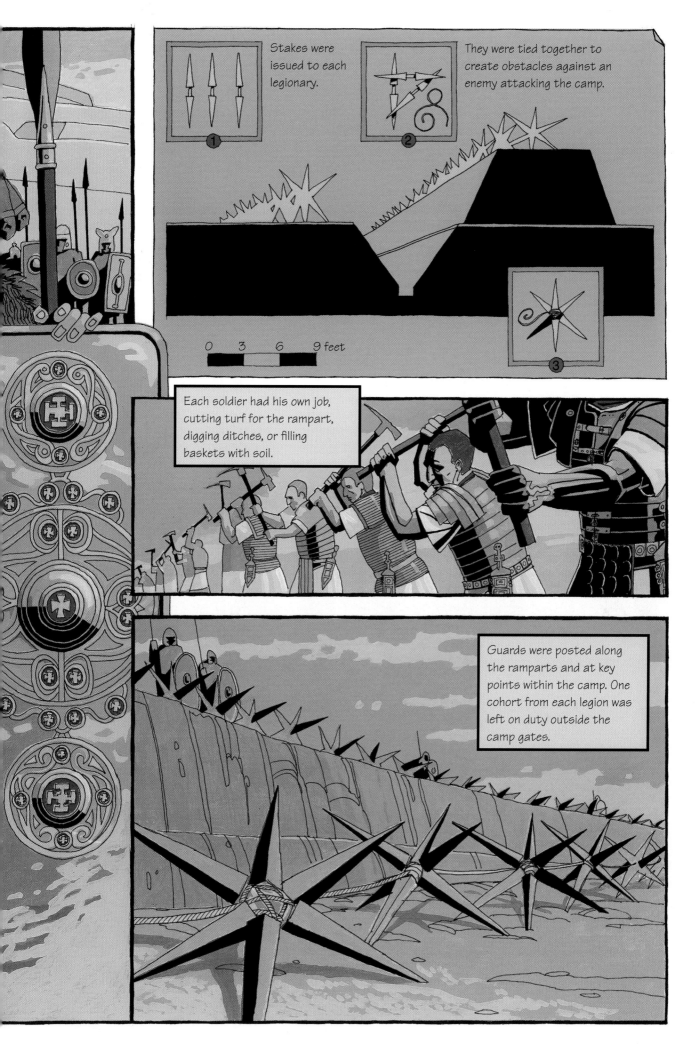

Stakes were issued to each legionary.

They were tied together to create obstacles against an enemy attacking the camp.

0   3   6   9 feet

Each soldier had his own job, cutting turf for the rampart, digging ditches, or filling baskets with soil.

Guards were posted along the ramparts and at key points within the camp. One cohort from each legion was left on duty outside the camp gates.

CATAPULT

Roman artillery was beautifully designed and constructed. The basic principles were simple.

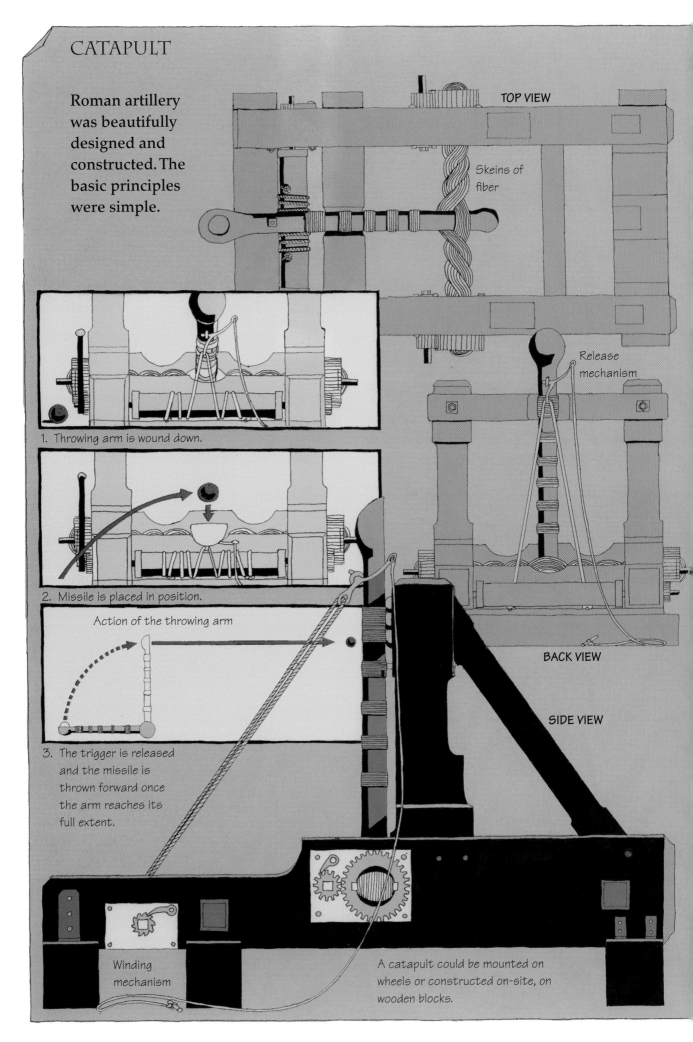

TOP VIEW

Skeins of fiber

Release mechanism

BACK VIEW

SIDE VIEW

1. Throwing arm is wound down.

2. Missile is placed in position.

Action of the throwing arm

3. The trigger is released and the missile is thrown forward once the arm reaches its full extent.

Winding mechanism

A catapult could be mounted on wheels or constructed on-site, on wooden blocks.

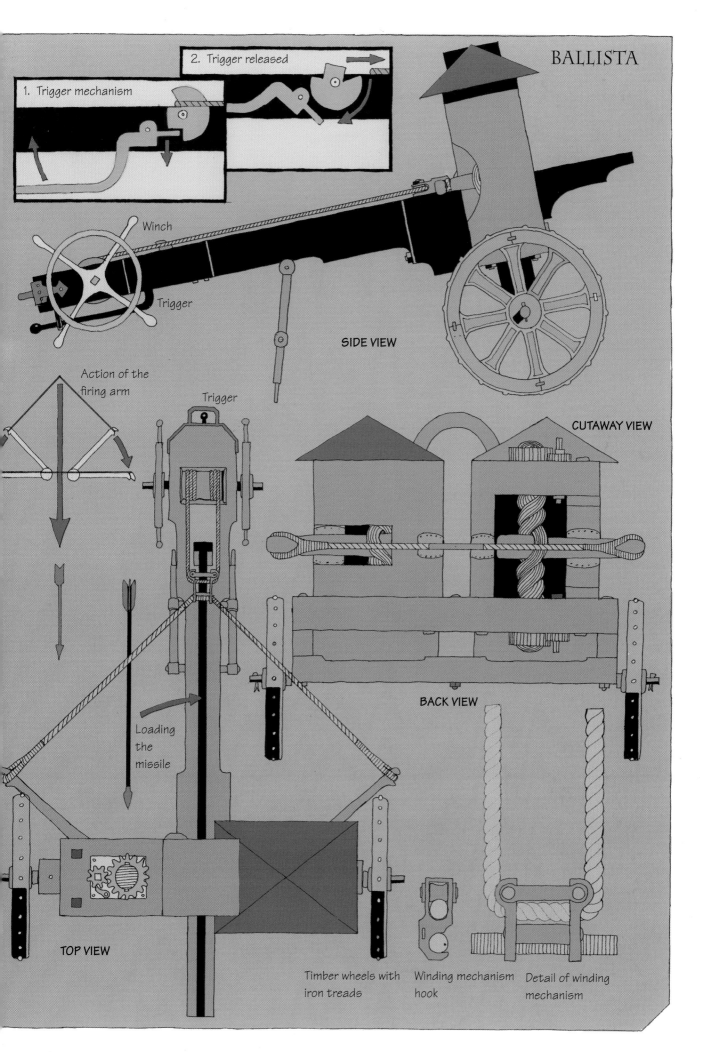

1. Trigger mechanism

2. Trigger released

BALLISTA

Winch

Trigger

SIDE VIEW

Action of the firing arm

Trigger

CUTAWAY VIEW

Loading the missile

BACK VIEW

TOP VIEW

Timber wheels with iron treads

Winding mechanism hook

Detail of winding mechanism

The army began its attack with throwing weapons. Ballistae fired heavy arrows over great distances. They were moved into position to provide long-range firing power. Weapons launched from ballistae had a range of up to 1,300 feet (400 meters). Archers provided covering fire for the infantry. For the enemy, the size and strength of the Roman army were often enough to force surrender, sometimes before the battle had even begun.

Others fought to the death.

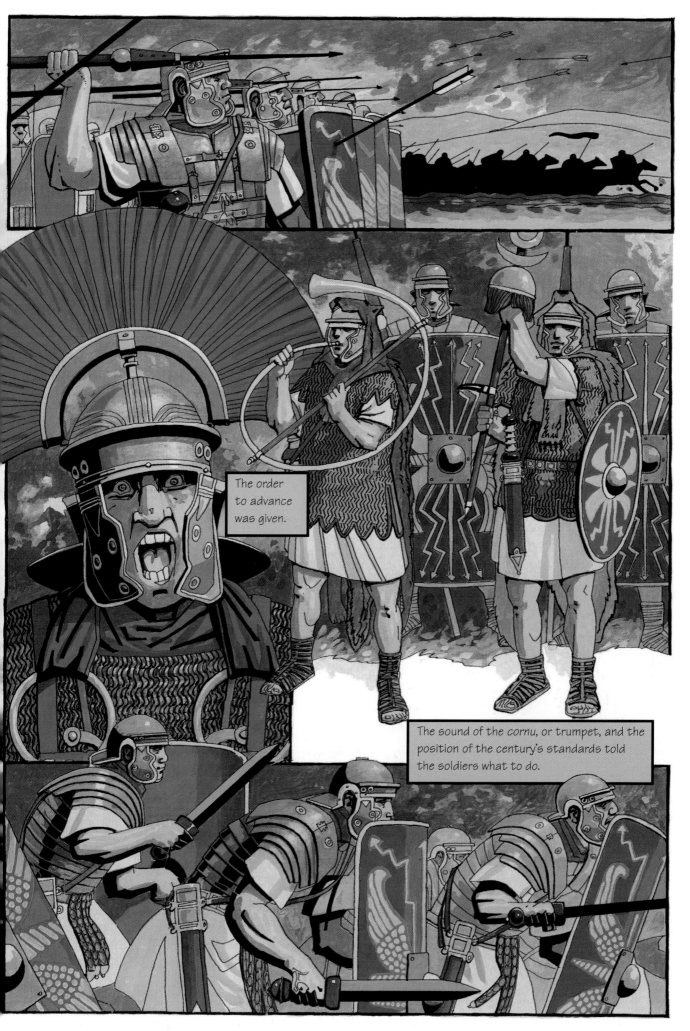

The order to advance was given.

The sound of the cornu, or trumpet, and the position of the century's standards told the soldiers what to do.

After a successful battle Roman cavalry often pursued and killed enemy survivors. Other enemies were, as a result, less likely to offer resistance and sometimes surrendered without bloodshed.

Roman casualties were carried to a tent field hospital, where emergency treatment took place. Roman army surgeons cleaned wounds with wine and used opium and alcohol as sedatives. Soldiers suffering from severe shock or blood loss and those with internal injuries were unlikely to survive. Wounded soldiers who did survive were transferred to a permanent camp to recover.

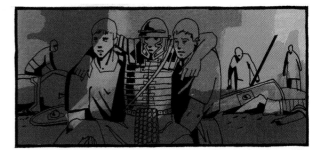

Roman cavalry pursued enemy soldiers, forcing them to retreat.

When an enemy town refused to surrender, the Roman army isolated it by setting up two lines of trenches and ramparts. The outer line prevented relief forces or supplies from reaching the enemy. The inner line linked forts built by the Romans. In between was a wide thoroughfare to allow the swift movement of troops around the fortifications. Building forts, siege works, and machines required massive amounts of timber, and whole forests were felled to meet the demand.

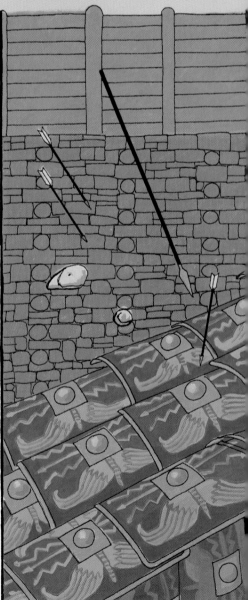

Once the decision was made to attack a town, heavy machines such as ballistae were drawn up. Siege catapults of varying sizes hurled stones through the air, crushing on impact whatever they hit. Stones were collected and laid at the feet of the catapult ready for use. The largest catapults could sling very large, heavy stones and made a terrifying noise.

A formation of legionaries with shields locked together was known as a *testudo*, or "tortoise." Such a formation, relatively protected from attacks from above, might lead the assault on the walls.

To terrorize its enemy, the army frequently killed most inhabitants of a defeated town, taking any survivors as slaves.

Bodies of the enemy were often left to rot on the battlefield.

Captives were sold to the slave traders that followed the army. Towns were plundered and the spoils usually shared in part with the men, although much of the captured booty was returned to Rome. Law and order were quickly restored, and the towns were rebuilt in the style of Roman towns.

In the Roman army, cowardice or desertion brought a harsh punishment. Soldiers guilty of these crimes were flogged or even put to death. Units that gave way in battle were made to live outside the camp on reduced rations, ostracized from their own community.

The bravest were rewarded. Common soldiers were awarded gold disks, *torques* (originally Celtic neck rings), or armbands. The *muralis* and *vallaris* gold crowns were awarded only to centurions or those of a higher rank.

After finishing their service in the army, soldiers were given grants of land and often settled in established communities.

An auxiliary with his diploma, or discharge from the army. He was awarded Roman citizenship.

After a great victory, there was a ceremonial parade through the Roman Forum. Captives were displayed, along with other booty, as the spoils of war. At the height of the empire, the Roman army's aggression, discipline, perseverance, and flexibility made it all but invincible. But in the end, all empires must crumble. No army alone can force an empire to endure forever.

BIBLIOGRAPHY

Adkins, Lesley, and Roy Adkins. *Introduction to the Romans*. London: Apple Press, 1991.

Branigan, Keith. *Roman Britain*. London: Reader's Digest, 1980.

Burrell, Roy. *The Romans*. Oxford: Oxford University Press, 1991.

Butterfield, Moira. *Going to War in Roman Times*. London: Franklin Watts, 2000.

Coarelli, Filippo. *Monuments of Civilization: Rome*. New York: Madison Square Press, 1972.

Connolly, Peter. *The Cavalryman*. Oxford: Oxford University Press, 1988.

_____. *The Legionary*. Oxford: Oxford University Press, 1988.

Connolly, Peter, and Hazel Dodge. *The Ancient City: Life in Classical Athens and Rome*. Oxford: Oxford University Press, 1998.

Cunliffe, Barry. *The Roman Baths at Bath: The Official Guide*. Bath, England: Archaeological Trust, 1993.

Dal Maso, Leonardo B. *Rome of the Caesars*. Florence, Italy: Bonechi, 1999.

Dando-Collins, Stephen. *Caesar's Legion*. New York: John Wiley & Sons, 2002.

Gibbon's Decline and Fall of the Roman Empire. Abridged and illustrated. London: Bison Books, 1979.

Gilliver, C. M. *The Roman Art of War*. Gloucestershire, England: Tempus Publishing, 1999.

Goldsworthy, Adrian. *Roman Warfare*. London: Cassell & Co., 2000.

Graham, Frank, and Ronald Embleton. *Hadrian's Wall in the Days of the Romans*. Newcastle-upon-Tyne, England: Frank Graham, 1984.

Hall, Jenny, and Ralph Merrifield. *Roman London*. London: Museum of London, 2000.

James, John, and Louise James. *Digging Deeper into the Past: The Romans*. Oxford: Heinemann, 1997.

Macdowall, Simon. *Germanic Warrior 236–568 A.D.* Warrior series, 17. London: Osprey Publishing, 1996.

Newark, Tim, and Angus McBride. *Barbarians*. Hong Kong: Concord Publications, 1998.

Peddie, John. *The Roman War Machine*. London: Sutton Publishing, 1994.

Peterson, Daniel. *The Roman Legions Recreated in Colour Photographs*. Europa Militaria Special, no. 2. London: Windrow and Greene Ltd., 1992.

Rankov, Boris. *The Praetorian Guard*, Elite series, 50. Oxford: Osprey Publishing, 1994.

Roberts, Timothy R. *Ancient Rome*. New York: Metro Books, 2000.

Simkins, Michael. *The Roman Army from Hadrian to Constantine*. Men-at-Arms series. Oxford: Osprey Publishing, 1979.

_____. *The Roman Army from Caesar to Trajan*. Men-at-Arms series. Oxford: Osprey Publishing, 1984.

Simpson, Judith. *Ancient Rome*. Melbourne, Victoria, Australia: Allen & Unwin, 1997.

Watson, G. R. *The Roman Soldier*. Ithaca, N.Y.: Cornell University Press, 1969.

Wilkinson, Philip. *What the Romans Did for Us*. London: Boxtree, 2000.

Windrow, Martin, and Angus McBride. *Imperial Rome at War*. Hong Kong: Concord Publications, 1996.

INDEX

ENEMIES OF ROME

Quadi warrior
First to second century A.D.
Germania

Sudanese tribal warrior
Second century A.D.
Africa

Tanukhid warrior
Fourth century A.D.
Arabia

Celtic light infantryman
First century B.C. to first century A.D.
Britannia

Gallic warrior
Third to second century B.C.
Gallia

Gallic warrior
52 B.C.
Gallia

Parthian horseman
A.D. 260
Parthia